Right the Vision:

Messages for the Mirror

Move from Affirmation to Manifestation

Legena S. Crawford

Cover Design: Immeasurably More Consulting Services, LLC.

Interior Design: Impactful Publishing, LLC.

ISBN: 978-1-7330887-2-5

Dedication

This book is dedicated to my husband, son, mom, family, and friends for encouraging me to take another look in the mirror to see who I REALLY am.

This book is also dedicated to those who hate the mirror or have difficulty seeing who God made you to be. Dear friends.... look again!

TABLE OF CONTENTS

TABLE OF CONTENTS

TABLE OF CONTENTS

Right the Vision

When we look in the mirror, we see a distorted view. How many times have you thought you looked one way and stopped to take another look in the mirror, and the vision you thought you saw was totally different? It is at this point you are not sure what to think. Could it be that it's not what you see that is distorted but how you see it and think about it? Could it be that you need to 'Right the Vision?'

Mirrors

At some point in life, we have all looked in a mirror. It may have been to look for flaws or focus on our features. It may have been to check our makeup or to capture that one last look or admiration before we present ourselves to the world for the day. Whatever the case, we have glanced at the mirror.

For many of us, we have been told to take a look in the mirror if there is something "wrong" with us. This implies that the mirror will reveal things we need to change and help us gain insight into things others may not like about us.

There are those who see the mirror as their friend and those who make it a point to avoid mirrors at all costs. This object is a constant reminder of what they need to correct or don't like about what or who they see.

For years I hated looking in the mirror! It was because the world had told me that I was fat and ugly, which led me to the sport of comparison. For years I blamed the mirror for showing me a person and things I did not like. However, as years progressed, I realized it was not the mirror that was my issue but what I saw or didn't see when I looked at it. Often, we fail to understand life and abuse the things around us that were meant to be tools to aid us in life. The mirror is one of those misused and abused tools.

The word *mirror* is a mid-13th century word that historically has roots that mean the following:

- A surface that is polished to reflect the image of an object.

- To admire and wonder at or to observe and watch and consider.

- A model or example.

Through the examination and revelation of this word, could it be we have been looking '*in*' and '*at*' mirrors the wrong way? This book intends to help reshape the mind and fully understand who and what we see. As you journey through these pages, allow your mind, body, and spirit to be renewed and rejuvenated as you take another look in the mirror. Your next look will take you down the path of affirmation to confirmation for the experience of full manifestation.

As you journey through these messages, take some time to grab a dry erase marker, pencil, or pen and find a dedicated surface. Possibly a mirror (car, bathroom, etc.), dry erase board, refrigerator, index card, sticky note, or counter to write these messages. When you write them, they will become an integral part of you and your day!

"I walk in the Boldness of who God created me To Be."

- When I look in the mirror, I see *"the me"* God created. I see the one who walks in confidence and courage. I am willing to be bold and take risks.

I WILL.......

_____

_____

_____

_____

Notes:

_____

_____

_____

_____

_____

_____

_____

_____

_____

"Today is a great day because I Serve a great God!"

- When I look in the mirror, I can either choose to see all my flaws or see that I am made in the image of a great God.

I WILL.......

_____

_____

_____

_____

Notes:

_____

_____

_____

_____

_____

_____

_____

_____

"While I'm Worshipping, God is Working."

- When I look in the mirror, I am reminded of the need not to worry about what I can't control. I trust that God is working everything out for me.

I WILL.......

_____

_____

_____

_____

Notes:

MM4

"My Life is a Thank You Note to God."

- When I look in the mirror, I am reminded that I am not here by accident. The way I live my life is how I tell God 'THANK YOU!'

I WILL.......

_____

_____

_____

_____

Notes:

"Spend time with HIM before you Spend time with THEM."

- We often wake up and immediately begin to think through our day. When our first conversation is with God, the other conversations will automatically fall in place.

I WILL.......

_____

_____

_____

_____

Notes:

"*God is turning my mistakes into miracles!*"

- There are times we hesitate to look in the mirror because we are reminded of the mistakes we've made in life. Be reminded that there is no mistake too big for God.

I WILL.......

_____

_____

_____

_____

Notes:

_____

_____

_____

_____

_____

_____

_____

_____

_____

"I Can do this with God's Help."

- When we look in the mirror, we often think the person looking back at us must be able to do EVERTYHING alone. We often forget if God gave us the ideas, He will give us everything we need, including His help.

I WILL.......

_____

_____

_____

_____

Notes:

"I will Take Time to Acknowledge how I Feel."

- Often when we look in the mirror, we are looking to fix something. Could it be when we look in the mirror, the need may not be to 'fix' something but to 'face' something instead?

I WILL.......

_____

_____

_____

_____

Notes:

"Keep Calm and Do It!"

- Time spent in the mirror often lends to time for self-talk. Instead of spending this time to confirm worry and doubt, use this time to convince yourself to remain calm, cool, and composed because you have things to do and goals to accomplish.

I WILL.......

_____

_____

_____

_____

Notes:

"I will Recommit to the God in me."

- As we wake to each brand-new day, a look in the mirror is another opportunity to recommit or cosign again to who God has called you to be. The mirror is a beautiful reminder of the fact that we are made in His image.

I WILL.......

_____

_____

_____

_____

Notes:

_____

_____

_____

_____

_____

_____

_____

_____

_____

"I will Make the Most of my Time...Daily."

- The fastest way to reduce your level of productivity is to waste time. Often, we complain about how much time we DON'T have. Wouldn't it be wise to use the time we talk about NOT having to increase our level of productivity?

I WILL.......

_____

_____

_____

_____

Notes:

_____

_____

_____

_____

_____

_____

_____

_____

"It's hard to Balance a Blessing and a Burden."

- Often, we are tired and feel out of alignment but not sure why. We may not recognize it, but it could be that in trying to balance life, we are trying to balance the blessings and the burdens. More often than not, it's the burdens that tilt the scale.

I WILL.......

_____

_____

_____

_____

Notes:

_____

_____

_____

_____

_____

_____

_____

_____

"I am the Example!"

• Often, we spend our days looking for others to compare ourselves to or pattern ourselves after. Could it be why we have difficulty satisfying our needs because we are the example?

I WILL.......

_____

_____

_____

_____

Notes:

_____

_____

_____

_____

_____

_____

_____

_____

"Life is going to Happen, so you might as well Live."

- We waste time worrying about what MIGHT or MIGHT NOT happen. The trouble with this is understanding that life is going to happen. So why not be intentional about enjoying every moment.

I WILL.......

Notes:

"I am the Face of Grace."

- A simple glance in the mirror can be life changing. It is a quick reminder that we are to operate in humility as we are the recipients of the favor of God that we don't deserve.

I WILL.......

_____

_____

_____

_____

Notes:

"I will Surround myself with Faith Walkers and not Doubt Talkers."

- The mirror is a reminder that you will spend more time with yourself than anyone else. The other people you choose to honor your space should have the same mindset that supports your faith and not contribute to your doubt.

I WILL.......

_____

_____

_____

_____

Notes:

_____

_____

_____

_____

_____

_____

_____

_____

_____

"I'm grateful that my History is connected to His Story."

- The mirror is a reminder that my past has already been covered by the blood of Jesus, which makes my present and future worth living.

I WILL.......

_____

_____

_____

_____

Notes:

"My Purpose Dictates my Preferences."

- The mirror is a reminder that I was created for a purpose. The decisions and choices I make each day should reflect that God prefers me.

I WILL.......

_____

_____

_____

_____

Notes:

_____

_____

_____

_____

_____

_____

_____

_____

_____

"A Crisis will always Remind me who Christ is."

- There are moments in life that may cause us to hit the panic button. A quick glance in the mirror is a reminder that we are not alone, and the power of Christ will show up in our crisis.

I WILL.......

_____

_____

_____

_____

Notes:

"I Choose to Pray for others and not Prey on them."

- It's sometimes easy for the enemy to convince us to *"get back"* at those who hurt and humiliate us. A real sign of spiritual maturity is to use the time of plotting to *prey* actually to *pray*.

I WILL.......

_____

_____

_____

_____

Notes:

"Be Mindful of what you Say After you Pray."

- As we encounter life, it is often easy to forget our prayers. We must be intentional not to allow the enemy to hinder our prayers by 'tricking' us into saying the opposite of what we prayed.

I WILL.......

_____

_____

_____

_____

Notes:

_____

_____

_____

_____

_____

_____

_____

_____

_____

"No matter how much I have LEFT, God will always find a way to make it RIGHT."

- Sometimes we refuse to look in the mirror because it reminds us how much we have lost. The mirror should serve as a reminder that if we are living, God can take what we have left and cause it to be the right moments in life.

I WILL.......

_____

_____

_____

_____

Notes:

"While my Blessing is being Prepared for me, I'm being Prepared for my Blessing."

- There are times we think God has forgotten about the prayers our heart desires. We must be encouraged and know the blessing has already been prepared in these times, and God is simply preparing us for the blessing.

I WILL.......

_____

_____

_____

_____

Notes:

_____

_____

_____

_____

_____

_____

_____

_____

"I'm going to look and live like I belong to God."

• Often, we check the mirror to make sure we have pinpointed the look of our choice or the latest trend. The reality is we should take time to look in the mirror to make sure we look like Him.

I WILL.......

_____

_____

_____

_____

Notes:

_____

_____

_____

_____

_____

_____

_____

_____

"Life is to be Lived and not Loathed."

- There are times when life happens, causing us to loathe or hate where we are the experiences we go through. These times are for remembering we are to live life and not allow life to live us.

I WILL.......

_____

_____

_____

_____

Notes:

_____

_____

_____

_____

_____

_____

_____

_____

"I will Envision the life I Desire, then Do what it takes to Live it Out."

- It's often difficult to execute a plan without seeing it. It is imperative to spend time with God to see the life He has already planned out for you.

I WILL.......

_____

_____

_____

_____

Notes:

_____

_____

_____

_____

_____

_____

_____

_____

"Life is too Precious and Valuable not to live Authentically."

- Most people spend their life to impress others. When this happens, we lose time being who we truly are and living the life we were called to live.

I WILL.......

_____

_____

_____

_____

Notes:

_____

_____

_____

_____

_____

_____

_____

_____

_____

"Is the real me showing up, or am I sending my representative?"

- A look in the mirror often shows a stranger because we have spent so much time sending our representative to live out the day. Life is meant for you to live, not your representative.

I WILL.......

_____

_____

_____

_____

Notes:

_____

_____

_____

_____

_____

_____

_____

_____

_____

"When you are feeling down, remember you can always look up."

- When feeling down about life, our body language reflects our feelings. We tend to unintentionally hold our heads down to reflect our mood. A quick fix and a reminder are to look towards the heavens, which will lift your spirit and your head.

I WILL.......

_____

_____

_____

_____

Notes:

"If God has given me the Keys, I won't let the devil Drive...or make him a Passenger."

- Often, we let our guard down when we think *"life is good."* It's during these moments the enemy sees our distraction by success and decides to convince us to let him drive or at least hitch a ride. Don't fall for the Okie-Doke!

I WILL.......

_____

_____

_____

_____

Notes:

_____

_____

_____

_____

_____

_____

_____

_____

"When I fill my space with worship, the enemy has no place to sit."

- The enemy is always looking to reside where we are because he hates to hear our worship and admiration for God; what better way to keep him away than to fill the rooms of life with worship!

I WILL.......

_____

_____

_____

_____

Notes:

_____

_____

_____

_____

_____

_____

_____

_____

_____

"It's Okay to be You because You are the Only One who Knows how to Do It."

- So much time is wasted trying to be like others and allowing others to tell us who we are instead of listening to who God created us to be.

I WILL.......

_____

_____

_____

_____

Notes:

"Don't allow the enemy to Diminish the Excitement about your Assignment...

Stay Focused!"

- We are distracted by little or low applause by people we care about or deem as our supporters. It's the enemy's way of distracting us from being excited about what God is doing through us.

I WILL.......

_____

_____

_____

_____

Notes:

_____

_____

_____

_____

_____

_____

_____

_____

_____

"I will not allow a Messy Mouth to Manipulate the Manifestation of my Miracles."

- When we have made up our minds to believe God, the enemy will try to distract us with the use of idle words. Words can either assist in creating a mess or miracles.

I WILL.......

_____

_____

_____

_____

Notes:

_____

_____

_____

_____

_____

_____

_____

_____

"I won't Abort the Process simply because Others can't See my Progress."

- There are mirror moments when we look and get sidetracked because we gauge our progress based on what others see or say. Remember, the process is YOURS.

I WILL.......

_____

_____

_____

_____

Notes:

_____

_____

_____

_____

_____

_____

_____

_____

"A part of the Healing Process is allowing Exposure to Lead to Closure."

- A major hindrance to healing is often our fear of exposure. It is difficult to heal what we won't allow to be revealed. The revelation is not meant to bring shame but to assist in the healing in His name.

I WILL.......

_____

_____

_____

_____

Notes:

_____

_____

_____

_____

_____

_____

_____

_____

_____

"It's difficult to REIGN if you haven't experienced some RAIN."

- Although we don't like it, rain is what helps plants grow. It's rain that helps cool the earth, and its rain that allows animals to quench their thirst so they can live. These scenarios serve the same purpose in our life. It's rain that causes us to lead from a place of God's authority.

I WILL.......

_____

_____

_____

_____

Notes:

_____

_____

_____

_____

_____

_____

_____

_____

"It's Okay to Reset without Regret."

- Often, a mirror moment will cause us to think about the need to press life's reset button. It is also that moment that regret can settle in and cause us to feel guilty about the need to do so. There is maturity in knowing when it's time to reset and begin again.

I WILL.......

_____

_____

_____

_____

Notes:

_____

_____

_____

_____

_____

_____

_____

_____

"You don't need the Permission from others to Believe God."

- Often, we look to others for permission to live. This need for permission can also affect our desire to believe God. Remember, people will only allow you to go as far as their faith will take them. Go ahead and believe God!

I WILL.......

_____

_____

_____

_____

Notes:

_____

_____

_____

_____

_____

_____

_____

_____

"A New Day doesn't begin with your feet, but it Begins with Your Mind."

- We have been conditioned to believe that the movement of our feet is what gets us from one level to the next. Before we even move our feet, we must make up in our mind the need to move at all.

I WILL.......

_____

_____

_____

_____

Notes:

_____

_____

_____

_____

_____

_____

_____

_____

_____

"If you are Still Going, it means you are Stronger than you Think."

- There are life moments that can cause us to think that we cannot go any farther. The enemy wants us to believe we are done, have lost all hope, and cannot move forward. If you are getting up every day and able to breathe and pray, you are much stronger than you think.

I WILL.......

_____

_____

_____

_____

Notes:

"Just because you had to Start Over doesn't mean you Failed. It means you were Smart enough not to keep going in the Wrong Direction."

- We often allow others to define what failure is to us. The real blessing is knowing you need to begin again, and you refuse to continue in the wrong direction.

I WILL.......

_____

_____

_____

_____

Notes:

_____

_____

_____

_____

_____

_____

_____

_____

_____

"When it comes to the Abundant Life, your Obedience to God will always Override your Opinion."

- Mirror moments often lead us to believe our opinion matters about what God is calling us to do. Our obedience to His plan will ALWAYS outweigh our opinion.

I WILL.......

_____

_____

_____

_____

Notes:

"When you Focus on the Enemy, your Mistakes become Failures. When you Focus on God, your Mistakes become Lessons."

- The enemy desires to consume your thoughts and make you think making a mistake is the end all be all, and there is no way to recover. Fix your focus on God and allow Him to show you the lessons the mistakes were meant to teach you.

I WILL.......

_____

_____

_____

_____

Notes:

"Don't let your Biggest Hater be You!"

- Mirror moments can cause us to pinpoint EVERYTHING that is wrong with us. We pull out our inner and outer flaws, thus moving them from the mirror to our mouth. Whatever you do, don't allow yourself to be your biggest hater or worst enemy.

I WILL.......

_____

_____

_____

_____

Notes:

_____

_____

_____

_____

_____

_____

_____

_____

"Know which Buttons the Enemy likes to Press so you can Deactivate them."

- There is power in knowing your triggers. These are the same triggers the enemy will use against you. Know your triggers so you can deactivate them and render him powerless.

I WILL.......

_____

_____

_____

_____

Notes:

_____

_____

_____

_____

_____

_____

_____

_____

"If your Giving is mixed with Complaining, either you need to Check your Motive(s) or keep your Gift."

- There is a blessing in being able to give. Don't allow the enemy to trick you into complaining about giving as Jesus gave His all to and for us.

I WILL.......

_____

_____

_____

_____

Notes:

"Disappointment is the Result of Expectations without Communication."

- Mirror moments cause us to have conversations with others, including their responses and understanding of our expectations. The problem is our expectations have not been communicated. It is essential to share our expectations even if they don't prevail.

I WILL.......

_____

_____

_____

_____

Notes:

_____

_____

_____

_____

_____

_____

_____

_____

"Asking God to Change you doesn't mean you get to Dictate how He does it."

- Many of us are accustomed to being in control of EVERYTHING. We ask God to change us, and we want to decide how He will do it. Sorry to announce that God STILL knows best and STILL does things His way.

I WILL.......

_____

_____

_____

_____

Notes:

"Stop Exhausting Yourself trying to Prove a Point to People who Don't Care about the Point you are Trying to Prove."

- We often try to figure out why we are so exhausted. Could it be the need to prove we are right and the fear of being misunderstood? Get your breath back because people will be people.

I WILL.......

_____

_____

_____

_____

Notes:

"Don't allow Anyone or Anything to get in the way of Your Relationship with God."

- The person who gets in the way of our relationship with God most is the person in the mirror. Don't let you be the reason your relationship with God is halted.

I WILL.......

_____

_____

_____

_____

Notes:

"It's hard to walk in Authority when you won't Submit to it."

- A mirror moment will sometimes lend itself to the idea that we don't have to be submitted and are in complete control. This is precisely the moment we need to be reminded that we are to be submitted to God in everything, in every way and every day.

I WILL.......

_____

_____

_____

_____

Notes:

_____

_____

_____

_____

_____

_____

_____

_____

_____

"I Choose to Live life B.I.G!"

- The way we live life is up to the person in the mirror. Interestingly, some choose to live based on the size of the mirror in which they see themselves. Regardless of the size of your mirror, choose to live a B.I.G life... **B**elieving **I**n **G**od!

I WILL.......

_____

_____

_____

_____

Notes:

_____

_____

_____

_____

_____

_____

_____

_____

"I will not complain just because it's convenient."

- It's often easy to look in the mirror and speak negatively. We sometimes make a point to bring to the surface our shortcomings that can lead to many complaints. Be mindful of allowing complaints to flow so easily as there is someone who would love to have the life you live.

I WILL.......

_____

_____

_____

_____

Notes:

"Just because it's Simple doesn't mean it's not Impactful."

- Sometimes we get sidelined and distracted by comparison. These moments can push us into thinking *everything* we do must always measure up to the standards of others. This is a reminder that big things still come in small packages. Let the focus be sincerity and not size.

I WILL.......

_____

_____

_____

_____

Notes:

"It's hard to reach New Levels when You're still Entertaining Old Devils."

- We often forget the past is meant to propel us and not stagnate us. When this happens, it's easy to focus on irritant sources, thus turning *all* our attention in the wrong direction. This makes it hard to reach new levels while stuck tending to the past.

I WILL.......

_____

_____

_____

_____

Notes:

"It's Okay to Clap for Myself."

- A look in the mirror can remind some of the reality of being alone. The enemy wants to use these moments to make you feel like you must have the applause of others to move forward. Learn how to clap for yourself because you are NOT alone. God is right there with you.

I WILL.......

_____

_____

_____

_____

Notes:

_____

_____

_____

_____

_____

_____

_____

_____

"Just because I'm not in Someone's Circle doesn't mean I'm out of Shape."

- The world can sometimes make us feel like we must fit in with the trends to be accepted. Sometimes taking a step outside the circle can help reshape your life.

I WILL.......

_____

_____

_____

_____

Notes:

_____

_____

_____

_____

_____

_____

_____

_____

"I will be Solution-Driven and not Problem-Ridden."

- Often a look in the mirror will reveal problems that overshadow the joy of life. Be determined to seek God to live a life driven by solutions.

I WILL.......

_____

_____

_____

_____

Notes:

_____

_____

_____

_____

_____

_____

_____

_____

Notes:

_____

_____

_____

_____

_____

_____

_____

_____

ABOUT THE AUTHOR

Legena Crawford, a native of Savannah, Georgia, is a pastor, teacher, speaker, mentor, wordsmith, and organizational consultant. Her experience in ministry and education span over 25 years.

She is the Pastor of P.O.W.E.R Point Christian Ministries, founder of LSCM633, and The

P.O.W.E.R Experience, LLC. Her greatest joy in life is being a wife, mother, daughter and spending time with her family and friends. She is led by the thought, *"Life is a gift from God. What you do and how you live is a thank you note to Him."*

Other Works by Author:

Face Value: Is Who You See, Who You Really Get?